War Diary: Lebanon 2006

Rami Zurayk

Charlottesville, Virginia

Just World Books is an imprint of Just World Publishing, LLC.

All text © 2011 Rami Zurayk. All rights reserved. No part of this book may be reproduced or transmitted in any form or by any means, electronic or mechanical, including photocopy, recording, or any information storage retrieval system, without permission in writing from the publisher, except brief passages for review purposes. Visit our website at www.justworldbooks.com.

Cover design and typesetting by Jane Sickon for Just World Publishing, LLC.
Printed by BookMobile, USA, and CPI, UK.

Zurayk, Rami.
   War Diary: Lebanon 2006
by Rami Zurayk.
     ISBN-13 for e-book: 978-1-935982-08-1
     ISBN-13 for paperback: 978-1-935982-09-8

Contents

A Note on Maps	6
Author's Preface	7
War Diary: Lebanon 2006	13
Glossary	57
Publisher's Information Page	59

A Note on Maps
from the publisher

The World Health Organization published a detailed map, dated August 15, 2006, that showed the main dimensions inside Lebanon of the complex humanitarian crisis caused by Israel's attacks. It is available online here: http://bit.ly/nIErGP.

The *New York Times* has an interactive map that shows the main features of the war, on both sides, as it developed day by day: http://nyti.ms/nPKSnl.

A map showing the main areas of West Beirut and some portions of the southern Beirut Dahieh can be found here: http://bit.ly/n16F5G. The Dahieh is roughly the area that stretches south and east from the Sports Arena.

A well researched map published by Human Rights Watch showed the main areas of South Lebanon that Israel hit with cluster munitions—the vast majority of them fired after the ceasefire had been negotiated on August 11, 2006, but before it went into operation three days later. The map is on p.4 of this PDF: http://bit.ly/oTaniZ.

Author's Preface

On July 12, 2006, a unit from Lebanon's Resistance[1] led by Hizbullah attacked an Israeli patrol near the village of Aita al-Shaab in South Lebanon and captured two of the soldiers to exchange them for Lebanese prisoners in Israeli jails. This was not the first time the Resistance had captured soldiers with such a prisoner exchange in mind. But this time, Israel unleashed a war that clearly had been prepared long in advance. Lebanon was carpet-bombed from air, sea, and land. Much of its infrastructure was destroyed and most of the South as well as the Dahieh (Beirut's sprawling and heavily populated Southern suburb) were flattened. But the Israeli Army, for the first time in its history, was unable to enter Lebanon and hold its ground there. It suffered heavy losses, while causing extensive—mainly civilian—casualties with the wide and frequently indiscriminate bombing campaign that it maintained throughout the 33 days of the war.

Israel's military and political leaders spelled out that their principal war aim was to inflict such heavy punishment on Lebanon's citizenry that the citizenry would turn against the Resistance and demand its disarming and dismantling. Some in Israel raised this concept to the level of a 'doctrine', which they dubbed the 'Dahieh Doctrine'. (Most people in the international community noted that this mode of warfare, which necessarily involves intentionally inflicting harm on civilian populations, is actually a war crime.) But despite the high losses inflicted on the Lebanese population during the war the Resistance emerged intact, and therefore victorious. Indeed, the war ended up achieving exactly the opposite of what its authors had sought. The victory of the Resistance also hammered a significant nail into the coffin of George W. Bush's New Middle East.

At the time Israel's government under prime minister Ehud Olmert launched the war, many Israeli commentators noted that it was also designed, more broadly, to "re-establish the credibility" of Israel's military deterrent—the credibility of which had, they felt, been seriously dented after previous Israeli governments undertook one un-negotiated, unilateral withdrawal from South Lebanon in 2000, and another from Gaza in 2005. But the last few days of the 2006 war were, from the viewpoint of the Israeli military, a complete fiasco. Ground units sent into South Lebanon in the war's last days were ill-prepared for combat and many soon found themselves encircled and outfoxed by smart and well-prepared Resistance units. In the days after the war, Israel's political discourse was marked by a loud chorus of recriminations and finger-pointing. Both the Defense Minister and the Chief of Staff were forced to resign in humiliation. Almost immediately, the new Defense Minister, Ehud Barak, started planning for another war—one that would this time, he hoped, finally and definitively re-establish the credibility of Israel's military deterrent. That assault, in the form of 'Operation Cast Lead', was duly unleashed against the population of Gaza in December 2008. Once again, the intention was to inflict such harsh punishment on the population that they would turn against their local resistance movement: in that case, Hamas. And once again, the attempt failed. Taking their inspiration in good part from the resilience that the Lebanese Resistance showed in 2006, Hamas and its partners in Gaza also survived several weeks of Israeli assault from land, sea, and air and emerged with their governance structure badly dented but still intact.

At a broader level, the Israel-Lebanon war of 2006 provided important confirmation to many in the Arab world that the weak do not have to remain so forever and that it is possible, with the appropriate preparation and alliances, to successfully defy the dominant system even when those who run that system possess and are willing to use the most lethal and destructive kinds of modern weaponry. For those of us in the Arab Left[2] who many years earlier had become disillusioned and had stopped believing in the effectiveness of fighting the imperial ogre and in the possibility of reversing the balance of power, this was a major lesson that reverberated throughout the whole region. Five years after 2006, many of the activists who led the pro-democracy movements in Tunisia, Egypt, and elsewhere that made up the 'Arab Spring' said that, along with the resilience shown by Palestinian resistance movements, one of the factors that inspired them to stand up to their own countries' large and American-backed militaries was their memory of how the Lebanese Resistance had stood up to the Israeli military for over two decades—and most spectacularly, in 2006.

The Lebanese Resistance emerged in its currently recognizable form as a direct response to the large-scale assault against Lebanon that Israel launched in the summer of 1982 and the military occupation of one-third of the country that it maintained thereafter. By 1985, the strength of the indigenous Lebanese Resistance movement had pushed the Israeli forces to pull back from much of that occupied area. The Israelis consolidated their position in a broad band adjoining the border that Israel called the 'Security Zone'—though most residents of the region experienced the continuing, aggressive presence of the Israeli occupiers and their local Quisling forces from the South Lebanon Army (SLA) as the cause of massive and continuing insecurity. The prison that the Israelis and the SLA maintained in the south Lebanese town of Khiam acquired international notoriety as a center of many of the worst forms of torture and rights abuse.

But the Resistance continued to grow in strength, organization, and sophistication. During the 1990s, it was able to withstand a string of further serious large-scale assaults launched by the Israeli military—most notably, in 1993 and 1996— and to inflict serious and continuing damage on Israeli and SLA military outposts inside south Lebanon. By May 2000 the situation of the Israeli military and the SLA had become so untenable that Israel undertook the unilateral withdrawal from Lebanon referred to above. That withdrawal was seen as very humiliating for Israel—and it constituted a significant victory for the Lebanese Resistance, which became recognized and admired by most Lebanese citizens and by the whole Arab and Islamic World.

Soon after the withdrawal of May 2000, and clearly stung by the humiliation it had suffered at the hands of the Resistance, Israel initiated a new campaign to destroy it. Millennia earlier, Cato the elder had identified Carthage as an unending source of trouble for imperial Rome and called for its destruction in a speech to the Roman Senate in which he thundered "*Cartago delenda est*", "Carthage must be destroyed." In 2000, we entered the era of "*Resistencia delenda est*" in Lebanon. After conquering Carthage, the Romans plowed large quantities of sea salt into the fields that surrounded the city-state, killing the soil and rendering it infertile. Food production ceased, and Carthage never recovered. Millennia later, the Israelis tried to do the same thing in South Lebanon, this time using cluster bombs instead of salt.

By 2000, Washington's design for a New Middle East had become apparent to all. In Lebanon, some Leftist intellectuals started to emerge from their torpor. We fully understood what was at stake: True, the Resistance was constructed around a sectarian party, the Shi`a Muslim movement Hizbullah. But it was also true that the Resistance had provided a revolutionary model of opposition to the dominant world order, a model that defied the long-established notion that the Arabs are a defeated nation. We understood that the Resistance had been sentenced to death precisely because of that: Because it made the Arab people see ourselves differently, because it dispelled the clichéd image of the Arab as a vanquished people, and because it undermined the myth of the invincible Israeli-U.S. alliance. In brief, the Resistance gave us courage, self-respect, and hope. These are values that are highly undesirable in populations that must be dominated, especially in the New Middle East.

In 2004, the events in Lebanon started rapidly to escalate. Under pressure from the United States and some countries of Europe, the United Nations passed Resolution 1559 calling for the withdrawal of Syrian forces from Lebanon and the disarming of the Resistance. Members of the group close to Prime Minister Rafic Hariri were accused of having participated in drafting the resolution, which, if implemented, would lead to the end of the Resistance. In Lebanon, where mainstream politics cannot be separated from their sectarian context, the resolution was also seen as an attempt to remove power from the Shi`a, who had historically been marginalized but had discovered their strength with the successes of the Resistance. A large-scale clash seemed imminent.

In February 2005, Rafic Hariri was assassinated in circumstances that remain obscure. The country split down the middle, and on March 14, hundreds of thousands of people assembled in the city center calling for the withdrawal of Syria, which they accused of killing Hariri. The U.S.–promoted 'Cedar Revolution' achieved its first and only success. After 27 years of military presence and political domination, the Syrian Army left Lebanon.

Like the rest of Lebanon, the Left split in the middle. Some joined the ranks of the U.S.-supported alliance, which promoted neoliberal values and was allied with the neoconservatives worldwide. Others declared their support to the Resistance but expressed reservations concerning the sectarian nature of Hizbullah and its social and economical agenda.

Then in June 2006, while Lebanon was still feeling the effects of that internal turmoil, the war erupted...

Notes

1 "The Resistance" is the translation of *al-Muqawama*, the name we use to refer to the Islamic Resistance in Lebanon, which is predominantly Hizbullah but includes a brigade of non-Hizbullah fighters, many of whom are non-Muslim. The Resistance movement also includes other parties that are more secular, but their actions remain symbolic.

2 The term "Left" is used here to refer to people who may or may not be organized in a party structure. However, they share the following core principles: (1) They adopt class analysis as a tool to understand the world of humans and their interactions; (2) they understand the notion of balance of power and seek to reverse it; and (3) they aim to bring about freedom with equality and consider that one cannot exist without the other.

War Diary: Lebanon 2006

On July 12, 2006, I was standing on the balcony of my little house in Sinay, my village in South Lebanon, when the bombing started. It came from deep inland, and we could tell it was air raids and field artillery. Suddenly, Israeli fighter jets swarmed the morning skies. The neighbors brought the news: The Resistance had attacked an Israeli patrol near Ayta al Sha`eb, and it had taken two prisoners to swap for the Lebanese prisoners held in Israeli jails. Israel was in mad furor and was randomly bombing the South. Kids were distributing sweets at the crossroads to celebrate the success of the Resistance, but many people sounded worried, and the bombing was getting closer to my village. Around 2 p.m., we heard that the South had been the target of more than a hundred air strikes. I decided to go back to Beirut.

Very few people were on the road. I drove very fast, and it took me just over 15 minutes to get to the Zahrani overpass. A friend called to inquire about me. I answered that I was nearing Saida. At this moment, there was a huge explosion, and my car swerved from the force of the shock waves. Volutes of smoke billowed behind me.

Back home in Beirut, I watched the news on TV: Tens of villages had been hit, and thousands of people were leaving their homes to seek refuge in Saida or in Beirut. This is how I learned that I had narrowly escaped the air raids. Many people had died, people who, like me, were running away to the safety of the city.

The 33-day Israeli war on Lebanon had begun. I didn't know it was going to change my life.

The next day, I started this diary, which I kept on an almost daily basis. I sent parts of what I wrote to friends abroad and kept some entries for me. I did not write much about everyday news, as these events were covered by hundreds of reporters and beamed in real time all over the world. I wrote about my daily life and my personal reflections, my frustrations, my powerlessness, my anger, and my hopes. This journal evolved later into the Land and People blog.

July 13, 2006

I got into a fight over the phone with a friend, a rich woman from the Beirut suburb of Ashrafieh. She called yesterday evening to ask about me, as she knows I spend a lot of time in the South. I told her I had gotten back *in extremis*. She was very nice and I appreciated that she called. I called back this morning and she launched into a violent attack against the Shi`a and accused them of planning to take over the whole country. She kept shouting and shouting until I flipped and started shouting back. It didn't make me feel better.

There are thousands of displaced people from the South, and I'm looking to be of help. I have called a friend who is active in social-political work and offered my services in case they want to organize a relief operation. I'm waiting for an answer, hoping it will come soon. I'm going to fix my bike (as in bicycle). Then I'll be able to move freely in Beirut and in the country should things deteriorate further, as I expect them to do. My in-laws from Jordan are staying with us and they want to leave as soon as possible, before Lebanon is locked up. I'm trying to send my family with them so that I can be alone and able to move as I wish, but Muna is resisting.

The kids have been at home all day today, as we neither had the heart nor the will to leave: we were mesmerized by the news roll on TV and the pictures that were coming to us: burned cars, destroyed houses, and people. Sad people, angry people, poor people, clutching meager belongings and trying to flee the grips of death.

We're expecting raids on the southern suburbs of Beirut, as the Israelis have threatened, and Bush gave them the green light to "defend themselves" by killing us. That makes me laugh. That makes us all laugh. They do not know that life has no sense unless it is lived with pride, head up. And that we are all dead anyway. Dead the moment we are born. So earlier or later, what difference does it make?

July 14, 2006

My family is not going to Jordan. I tried to convince them but Muna is adamant on staying. This is rather unfortunate, but Muna is like that: fierce and determined when she knows that right is on her side. I hope she will change her mind. Her sister now lives with us as well as her parents who were visiting.

I can't describe the atmosphere at home. Four kids, three nannies, two older people, two anxious women and one angry son-of-a-bitch. Ah yes, and two dogs, one of which keeps pissing in the house.

I went out for an early run with the dogs on the beach this morning. It was eerie. There was no one in the streets. Gigantic smoke columns rose from the southeast, from the airport area and the suburbs. Ramlet el Baida was empty, even from the bums who spend the night there during the summer. There was one lone guy towards the northern end of the beach. He sat by the shore, drinking beer and chain smoking. He mustn't have been more than eighteen. Bella went to get a dose of caressing, and he kindly offered me a beer. I briefly considered sitting by him, smoking and drinking instead of trying so hard to keep a healthy envelope to a rotten soul.

Many people here are anxious about Lebanon and they should be. They are concerned about the time it would take to bring business back after this war ends, when it ends. They are worried about schools that will not open, businesses that will go bust, tourists who will fly away never to come back, and about the collapse of the economy. And they are right to be worried.

These people are like me. They fear losing their comfort, which is associated with the vibrant *souk* Lebanon has become. They can see their dreams shattered, their happiness threatened, their country dilapidated. Many have only recently returned to Lebanon from a long self-imposed exile brought about by the unending wars. They've really started to like it here, after power cuts disappeared, after running water became available, after bridges and highways were built, after clubs and restaurants opened so they could feel as if they were still in Paris, Rome, London or New York; and after private universities opened so that they could pay their way into "achieving their intellectual potential" and be the first in the long line for the few jobs available.

But there are other people in Lebanon. People who are not comfortable. People who cannot afford private education and have to settle for the free local university, and accept the fact that they will never be able to speak, read, or write English, the language of opportunities. People who have electricity just six hours a day. People who have no running water. People who only enter restaurants through the service door. People who have to tolerate the roughness of clients to keep a job and who have to laugh at their stupid jokes for a two dollar tip. People who do not have cars to drive on the new highways and who go to work in a minivan driven by an abusive man wearing a dirty undershirt. People who have never been to nightspots like Monot, Gemmayzeh and Solidaire, Pierre and Friends, La Voile Bleue, Pangea. People whose sister or daughter leave home sometimes in the evening to return the next day, telling them that she is sleeping at her friend's. But if she sleeps at her friend's, why only during the holiday season? And why all the make-up? And where does she get the money she gives her mother?

These people could not care less about the bourgeois Lebanon we live in. Their country is like their houses: ugly, degraded, stinky and windowless. What are we afraid the Israelis will destroy? The city center, the economy, the tourism? All of that means nothing to them. What we are afraid of losing was never theirs. It is ours, although they may have constructed it. And their lives count for very little in today's Lebanon.

July 15, 2006

Things were relatively calm last night, and the lull is continuing. This is a typical Israeli tactic: bomb civilian areas causing as many casualties as possible, as if to say "we mean business" and then give some time for a few civilians to get out of the target areas with little more than what they can carry in a bag. Then destroy everything. This is what they did during the 1982 invasion.

The problem is: where can all those people go? The Southern suburbs (Dahieh) are heavily populated by poor and lower-middle-class Southerners and Beka'ais. Those from the Beka'a have managed to get out and go back home. The Southerners, those with whom Israel has a score to settle, cannot go back South. They are condemned, like my friend T., to seek asylum in other areas of Lebanon, 'safe' areas because Israel will not bomb Christian or Druze areas (that is an Israeli tactic too, dividing a population by favoring some groups over others).

I say "condemned" because it really is a sentence: T. told me her story, which I also heard from many others. They tried to rent a house or a hotel room in the mountain resort of `Aley. They had to bear the heavy reproachful words, take the blame for all that is happening, as if they were the ones who were doing the destruction, and not the Israelis. They were harangued with political doctrines based on recognizing Israel as a super power and the need to make friends with it and with the Americans so that they "let us live."

This is what is happening with refugees elsewhere. When they arrive to a locality, people take sideways glances at them as they pass, their luggage piled up in the trunk of their bursting cars. They make sarcastic remarks about the large families, and tell them that things would have been easier were there not so many of them. They look at them as if they are dirty or infectious. They imitate their accents in exaggerated fashion, and then laugh at their own joke. Then they ask for exorbitant prices for a single room, or for a tiny flat, which they refuse to rent except by the year. The boldest of them admit it: "You have screwed the tourism season, now you're going to pay for it." The crummiest hotel rooms go for a hundred dollars a night; tiny studios without electricity or water are three thousand dollars for the season. But the insults come for free.

July 17, 2006

I have started working with the displaced. I don't know which is sadder: that there are so many displaced poor people or that the emergency support is so badly organized.

July 18, 2006

Yesterday, I met with people who are trying to organize emergency relief for about 10,000 families of refugees from the southern suburbs into West Beirut. I met with the people working on the ground and they confirmed what I had thought: it is mayhem. The displaced lack everything, and the Lebanese government is pussyfooting with the money they have promised to give the Higher Commission for Relief, and are only giving support to those who have sought refuge in Hariri schools. They are using the plight of hundreds of thousands of people to pull cheap political stunts. Anyway, I tried to convince the people I'm working with to start a fundraising campaign, and they have asked me to manage it. I really don't want that, primarily because I have no experience in mass fundraising.

I was called to a coordination meeting in Hayy el Lijaa, one of the poorest areas of Beirut. The office I was in looked as if it had been recently bombed, although the last time the area saw any bombing was in the late 1980s. There were tens of unshaven sweaty men in ill-fitting clothes. The streets were full of displaced families, cooling off in the summer night breeze. And you know what? They were cheerful. It felt as if they were actually having a fine time, socializing, smoking, analyzing, flirting, and showing off. I left to go to Ras Beirut, Beirut's 'intellectual hub.' There was no one in the streets. It was a totally deserted ghost town, people were hiding behind their heavy doors and their pulled curtains shading the 35 degrees Celsius heat. And this is the most secure neighborhood in Beirut. What are they afraid of? Go figure the human mind.

Muna's parents have left this morning to go back to Jordan. Her sister has been evacuated with the United Nations.

July 19, 2006

Muna now goes everyday to work in a center for displaced people with a group of health specialists from the American University of Beirut (AUB). Yesterday she came back depressed and with a terrible headache while I was holding high-level meetings in air conditioned rooms with the upper management of the disaster, people who couldn't even administer their own asses. This morning, she was ready to hit the street again.

July 21, 2006

Yesterday I called an old friend who is now in Broummana and he told me that a friend's father had passed away. In the church where they held the funerals I wanted to capture some spirituality while the poor guy who had died from a lightning strike of leukemia slept in his coffin. I tried hard to look for some remnant of faith, whatever faith, Christian, Muslim, Buddhist, anything, but found nothing. And when I scraped really deep in my soul to see if it was really empty, I felt I could really tear a hole in it and still find nothing. So I accepted the fact that I am an atheist looking very hard for some religious spirituality because it may make me feel better about the world, but finding nothing. Sometimes, I wish I could be a believer; it would make my life so much better. Especially during this war.

July 22, 2006

It is at times like these, when everything is collapsing, that I start wondering what is Lebanon and who are its people. I mean this is a place where half the population is rejoicing because Israel is bombing the other half! But then again, this is a place where the streets are still named after the generals who invaded the country and killed its people: Gouraud is one of them, a man who ordered the French army into South Lebanon to quell the insurrection against the French Mandate. The "Colonne Sud" carried out air raids on Bint Jubayl and executed freedom fighters such as Adham Khanjar long before the Israelis did similar things.

In Lebanon, fluency in the culture and the language of the colonizer or the powerful is considered a necessity. For the elites and much of the middle class, speaking Arabic is the exception rather than the norm. How did we internalize colonialism so much, especially since we were never formally colonized? I know that I can't claim to represent the Lebanese, but the story of how the French culturally colonized me may be worth documenting, especially since I was a very unlikely candidate. Or was I?

I was born at the end of the 1950s in a modest family. My father came from a very poor Shi`a family of South Lebanon, and, when he married my mother, he was a sports teacher in a government school. My mum's father was a well-off Sunni Beiruti trader who had divorced his wife leaving his two adolescent daughters and his very young son in the care of an evil stepmother. My mother and her siblings went to the French Lycée. At home, they were terrorized by the evil stepmother who made them toil and entertain their step-brother and sister. Eventually, my mum ran away with my father who had been hired to help her with Arabic for the Baccalaureate exam. My aunt, a couple of years younger, ran away to Ashrafieh where she lived with Christian friends, adopted the French way of life and became a kindergarten teacher in the Lycée. My uncle ran away into mental illness and remained a Muslim Arab. It was he who later on, during the 1975 war, taught me about our Arab culture and our heritage.

Of my entire mother's family, only her cousin who was studying to be a doctor, attended the wedding. Mixed Shi`a-Sunni marriages were still very rare, and marrying into poverty was a cardinal sin. My Frenchization started at babyhood and I am told that I spoke French before I spoke Arabic. I carried both my father's and my mother's chips on my shoulders: By cloning me from the babies in her favorite French magazines, she wanted to make it very clear that I was different from my father's family. For my father, it was as if my capacity to speak French fluently could cover up for his linguistic shortcomings. Of course, both of them wanted to prepare me better for life by giving me a head start, by endowing me with baggage that would distinguish me from the other people in my social class. The result was that I was shown around like a circus freak into our poor relatives' circles, who were awed by my gift for languages.

At age two, I was placed in daycare at the Sisters of Nazareth School in Ashrafieh, where my formation as a young Frenchman became institutionalized. At age four, my aunt enrolled me in the French Lycée. You have to realize that the Lycée was not an expensive school. It was just elitist. To be accepted into the Lycée, you had to be French. Preference went to those whose parents or siblings were studying or had been at the school. This automatically eliminated cross-fertilization and blocked the access to the newly emerging socio-economic classes. The colonial French, you see, are very sensitive to the *'nouveau-riches'* whom they greatly despise. These written rules for admission to the Lycée still apply today. As for the unwritten rules, they clearly favored those people who were 'culturally' French. The end result was that, throughout the fourteen years I spent at the Lycée, the distribution was always more or less like that: 15% French, 15% Lebanese Muslims, and 70% Lebanese Christians. And I was as French as any French student in my class. My mother and my aunt made sure of that by keeping a close watch on my accent, my vocabulary, and my choice of friends.

Lebanon was never really a French colony in the classical sense of the term. Lebanon was not Algeria, for instance. The French did not establish a mandate in Lebanon to plunder its resources and use them as raw material in their industrial and economic development. Neither did they ship hundred of thousands of Lebanese to serve as cheap labor in the building of the French economy. No, the French (and the British) split the Near East among themselves at the end of the First World War, when they shared the territorial loot of the Ottoman Empire.

Both powers had already been actively promoting their interests in Lebanon before WWI through their consuls (not unlike what the U.S. ambassador Feltman does today). The French consorted with the Maronites and the Brits with the Druze. The rest of Lebanon was considered to be made up of unthreatening appendages. Palestine was given to the Zionist Jews, Jordan and Iraq to the Hashemites who had helped during the war, and the Arabian Peninsula, where oil was still undiscovered, was left to the few mad explorers who created beautiful myths about the Bedouins.

The French saw Lebanon as the land of the Maronite Christians. But Mount Lebanon was not thought to be economically viable (the notion of service economy and sex tourism was not fully developed yet). So the French expanded the borders of the country to include fertile agricultural lands— Akkar, Jabal `Amel and the Beka'a. These regions came with the destitute people living in quasi-servitude in them. It was thought that they could serve as unskilled labor, servants or that they would remain peasants. In order to color the country with a veneer of modernity, the confessional system, which ensured that the privileges of the ruling classes would never be challenged, was adopted. Only those who were culturally Western were admitted to the ruling club.

It may be true that we were never colonized by the West in the literal sense of the word. But we have been, and continue to be, culturally colonized, with our full accord. It seems to be beyond us to stop and say: This has got to end! Not until we start respecting and trusting our own culture will we be able to earn the respect and the trust of others. After all, who wants to trust a people who do not have self-respect? Who will respect a people who believe that it will gain the esteem of the West by acting like pathetic buffoons? In today's Lebanon, we want to build a nation using someone else's culture. How can that be? You couldn't even build a company this way!

Endorsement by the West has its fringe benefits, of course. Look at Lebanon today, and I mean today: July 22, 2006. The last evacuees are leaving the country, carted off by their respective nations, fearing the terrible Israeli war machine. But who are those evacuees? For the most part, they are Lebanese citizens who are naturalized as American, Canadian, Australian, French, or British. The only difference between them and other Lebanese are the twenty-eight pages of an A6-sized document: their passport. This little book increases the value of their lives beyond that of the rest of their families, their friends, and their neighbors. Is that fair? Is that acceptable? Note, however that their blood will never have the same worth as that of the white westerners; they are just free riders today on the big bus that is taking the real Americans (and others) out of Lebanon. The proof? Easy. A whole family of Lebanese-Canadians (nine members) was buried under the rubble of their village of Aitaroun in South Lebanon by an Israeli air raid. Did the Canadians raise their voice? No. The same thing happened to a family of Lebanese-Germans in Nabatieh. Heard of it? No.

Nothing of what I am saying is new. It has all been addressed very adequately by hundreds of post-colonial analysts. Every taxi driver in Beirut knows that the U.S. is an imperial power, and that it wishes to control world resources, especially oil, by placing stooges at the head of the Arab (and other) regimes. What we realize less is how much we are impregnated by Western culture, which we conveniently call 'international' culture. What's international about Coca Cola or Madonna except the fact that you can find them marketed almost anywhere in the world? There is a more sinister aspect to this 'internationalization': our own image is now fabricated for us by Hollywood. The Arab image we have in our mind comes from there. Many people in Lebanon think of Arabs as camel jockeys and rag heads, and despise "them" and declare openly that they have no culture. History is also written by the western media: Watch CNN, BBC, read the *New York Times*, and other newspapers and magazines and you'll find a one-sided view of the events that are tearing up our region, often taken out of context. We find that the Lebanese who die do not have the same value as the Israeli casualties and worse of all, we believe it all and take it for granted and it becomes the unshakable premise of our thinking.

I have three children. They are named Thurayya, Ali-Usama, and Suha. Classical Arabic names. They are twelve, eight and six. Thurayya is the only one who can manage spoken Lebanese decently. The younger ones cannot speak Lebanese Arabic properly. I have to promise I will buy them presents if they speak Arabic for a whole day, something they have yet to achieve. When bombs fall around us, they huddle around me and cry and curse Israeli and American savagery. In English.

July 24, 2006

It's Sunday afternoon, the suicide hour. It must be strange to hear someone talk of suicide during a war as violent as the one we are living today. It is not strange it is sick. It feels as if I am ungrateful to what has been granted to me while dozens are dying every day in my close surroundings. I'm not really suicidal, I'm just very tired and my brain feels like something that has been boiled then bleached and passed through a blender. It must be the aftermath of the shock of the war.

Muna made an unexpected comment to me today. She said: "You know what's odd with you? Your response time to extreme events, like war or accidents or death is very slow. When we are all being shaken, you appear impervious and unaffected to anything that comes from the outside, until we all start to get out of the depression and go back to normal life. Then you start showing signs of weariness and breakdown. But by then you cannot benefit from our collective support system, because it is now operating at very low intensity. We have all gotten used to the new situation."

I don't know what all of this means. I'm really starting to get fed up.

Things were quiet in Beirut today. The Israelis are mostly dealing with the Beka'a, and they are busy destroying the private sector industry. What is the level of hate one must have when deciding to attack civilian economic targets. They are bombing dairy factories! What on earth? Tissue paper factories? How can these be strategic targets? Unless they are set on destroying the economy and punishing the country by bombing it, as they always threaten, 'back into the stone ages.' They did this in the West Bank after the second intifada, and this is what they are doing in Lebanon too.

In the meantime, the evacuation of the foreigners continues, as if they were preparing us for an assault to which only those whose blood is cheap need to be exposed. I know it is part of the psychological warfare, but it is quite incredible that the whole world is in league in this action. Especially, many of the Lebanese themselves. Yesterday, Nayla Moawwad was feeding arguments to the Israelis: "This is all made in Syria." And the rest of Lebanon: The 'socialists' of Jumblat: I've never seen a people so willing to collaborate with the Israelis. And the Hariri-ites, eternal Saudi clients, holding a bi-level discourse, cursing the Resistance with one side of their mouth while practicing one-upmanship on Arabism and the Palestinian cause with the other. Apparently a cleric in Saudi Arabia came up with a fatwa that it is a sin to help or to feel compassion with the Shi`a. In Beirut this is reflected by the sneers directed towards the hundreds of thousands of refugees who are at the mercy of the Beirutis. The government is delaying the distribution of aid coming from Arab countries. Yesterday, a Kuwaiti aid convoy was about to turn back from the Lebanese border as the customs wouldn't let it in! But the upside is that apparently the `Aounis are doing a really good job at helping the displaced. I don't know what to believe or trust anymore, I hope it is not a cheap stunt for popularity. Well even if it is, at least they are not wasting time on settling internal scores and being U.S. and Israeli stooges.

The situation is bad. It could go anywhere, even towards a regional war. The Israeli press is reporting that Israel would like a cease-fire but the U.S. is refusing. I don't know how true this is, but the U.S. certainly seems intent on another Iraq, this time using the Israeli army to avoid spilling U.S. blood. History will remember the U.S. as a nation of unequalled ruthlessness, and the rest of the world as mere colonies with varying degrees of self-rule. There are only a few countries, people, or nations still opposing their hegemony and I am proud to be a witness to that. I hope my family will survive unscathed. I do not care about myself. If I could send them to Jordan, I would go to the south and stay there. I need to be reunited with the fields, the hills, and the valleys.

I realize now that war is the normal state of affairs for me. I slide back into it effortlessly. I run in the empty streets every morning. Six to seven is the time when people are still unsure whether to get out of the house or not, when they wait and see, when the last explosions can still be heard and when the smoke and dust of the bombs hasn't settled yet. This is when I run. I went to the port today and then through the city center to Martyrs' Square and back through Bab Idriss and Clemenceau. I run with just my shoes and light shorts, and with Bella of course. People must think I'm mad, but so far no one has objected.

I expect things to get much worse as electricity and phone go away. I've checked the shelter, and it's reasonable, but only for a few hours.

July 25, 2006

Nothing new on the war front. The South is being destroyed and its people killed, and so is the Beka'a. Condoleezza Rice gave an ultimatum, and it looks like all hell might break loose in the next few days. We're now waiting for it; shelters are ready. What we hear is that the Americans will give free hand to the Israelis to bomb heavily till Sunday, at which time they will check again to see if we are ready to yield or not. If not, they will probably go for another week, and so on until we either give up or they finish their bombs. And the whole world not only watches, but blames us! We do not want to be treated as victims; this is a war against a ruthless enemy and we should know from its past that it is ready for anything and that it acts in impunity, because this is how it was created: by an injustice sanctioned by the UN and the West. But to treat Israel as a victim! Come on! Look at the body count for God's sake!

A friend sent a message from France to inquire about our safety. I wrote back saying we are holding on, and if we are to die we will do so proudly. She accused me of being mad and of supporting a religious obscurantist movement. As a leftist, she added, you should know better. She is a member of the French socialist party.

I despise most of the European left with its pervasive hypocrisy. I support the Resistance against the Israelis, while I do not agree with Hizbullah's social and economic agenda. This is a religious party with conservative views. But today, they fight Israel, and they are among the very few people in the world who are still holding their heads high and have not joined the other sheep in the great American flock. And that is admirable, this refusal to give in, this stand-offishness when you know that you have only the tiniest chance of survival but you still do it because dying with pride is better than living like rats. Look at the fate of the Native Americans at the hand of the founders of white America. They were systematically eradicated so that the settlers could take all their land and create a prosperous nation. Some Native Americans stood up and fought. They were all killed. Those who did not were parked into reservations where their descendants are today marginalized, neglected, and prey to alcoholism. And then the U.S. system created Hollywood images and fed them to their ignorant audiences in order to convince them that it was the Native Americans' fault. Did you know that scalping was invented by the white settlers who got paid for every scalp, as they got later on paid for every coyote's tail when the time came for their eradication? That's what we are to them: vermin. And in the same way as there are now selective pesticides that cause less environmental damage while inflicting maximum losses on the pest population, so has the U.S. and Israeli military arsenal improved. Yesterday, the US gave Israel 1,000 'intelligent' bombs, state of the art military toys capable of penetrating thirty meter deep bunkers. Might as well stay in my eighth floor apartment when they bomb.

July 26, 2006

It's my forty-eighth birthday today, and I have asked family and friends to withhold greetings and celebrations until land and people are liberated. This might take a while as my indicator of liberation is the creation of a democratic and secular state in Palestine. This gives me a solid ideological excuse to avoid being reminded of how old I am.

I've always had mixed feelings about birthdays. They are a good occasion to be the center of interest, and I love that, but they also remind me of how quickly time passes when one is over forty. I am unavoidably moving with giant steps towards half a century, which, as we all know, is when all of man's vital functions break down. I hate aging. And I am not taking it graciously. I am no philosopher capable of detaching himself from the lowly pleasures of material life.

My father, another great lover of life, told me that he worshipped Ernest Hemingway because he killed himself when he felt he was getting too old for hunting, fishing, drinking, and womanizing. My father was very impressed by the alleged story of how Hemingway had decided that he would kill himself when he'd stop being able to shoot accurately in the center of a target board. My father kept threatening that this is what he would do to himself. But he never was a big hunter, just a frantic womanizer, and since the discovery of Viagra, he can always claim that his shooting is still acceptable. I don't think he'll kill himself any more: in the past eight years he has fought off prostate cancer and leukemia, and had triple bypass surgery. I don't think he'll kill himself at eighty-two. A few weeks ago he told me: "You know Rami, the problem with aging is that I feel the same inside. I haven't changed a bit since I can remember being." The French author, François Mauriac (who is now dead) said something like that: *"Je me sens pareil à ce que je fus toujours au point de croire que la vieillesse n'existe pas."* I feel I am so similar to what I have always been that I sometimes believe that getting old does not exist.

And as I seem to have come to quotations, here's one that comes from a surprising book I have just discovered in one of the rare used-book shops of the city, located near Jeanne D'Arc Street in Hamra. I am talking about the marvelous "Citadelle" by Saint Exupéry which he must have written under the influence of LSD. I have read about 100 pages so far, and it seems to be the memoir of a Berber tribal chief confronted with the decadence of his empire. It feels like the scenario of a comic strip published by the "Humanoides Associés" in the mid eighties. The plot is not very coherent, but one can find in it pearls of wisdom. Here's one about anniversaries:

"And time is to rites as space is to a dwelling. For it is good that the time that passes does not seem to wear us and waste us, like a handful of sand, but to accomplish us. It is good that time becomes a construction. Thus I walk from feast to feast, and from anniversary to anniversary, from harvest to harvest, as I walked as a child, from the Council room to the resting room, in the thick of my father's castle, where every step had a meaning." Amen.

July 27, 2006

I saw Lebanon on TV last night, and I did not like it one bit. It was in a TV program on LBC. A patronizing egghead had organized a debate among youth from all major Lebanese political parties. I have never seen so many stereotypes come true: There was the skinhead-in-suit from the Lebanese Forces; the fat, sweaty, hairy-chested Hariri-ite man; the smartly dressed, attractive

Aouni girl; the unshaven, slightly emaciated Hizbollah guy, floating in badly cut clothes; the vociferous Jumblati trying to be politically ubiquitous; and an absolutely stunning woman who I suppose represented the Monot crowd. The LF guy spoke local Lebanese Arabic peppered with French words, and blamed it all on Iran. The Hariri-ite was trying to be a smartass by supporting the Resistance, but only when it is not resisting. The Aouni girl was trying to be detached about it all. The Hizbullah guy spoke impeccable Arabic but was on a different planet while the Jumblat guy was on all planets at the same time without losing his mountain accent. I can't remember what the woman from Monot said. They were repeating, with the insecurity of their youth, the same stale arguments peddled by their confessional leaders. It was so painful I had to watch to make sure that there is no future for this nation.

This morning, N., an acquaintance who thinks of himself as a Lebanese Christian Maronite intellectual, and who is in reality rather a bigot, called me to tell me he was near AUB. We had coffee together, and I understood that he was on a mission to ask me to convince the Shi`a leadership to stop and introspect and realize that they are suffering from severe delusion and to go back to being normal human beings and citizens of the world. I kid you not. He had approached me because, he said, he "knew I was open-minded and that I could, like him, understand." He made unwittingly tons of racist and prejudiced statements, but he was right on one thing: The majority of the Shi`a (those who support the Resistance) really are on a totally separate wavelength from the rest of the world, especially the rest of Lebanon.

I gave him my speech on the necessity to fight oppression wherever it is found, and about our moral duty as human beings to combat tyranny and discrimination. He spoke about the Hariri plan which in his view was to annex Lebanon to Saudi Arabia and put it under the rule of the Sunnis. He told me how bad and petty the Sunnis are and how generous and kind hearted the Shi`a are. I said he should convert to Shi`a. I made a foolish attempt at raising the poverty issue, and the neglect of the marginal areas, especially the Shi`a ones, by the great Hariri economic development project. He maintained that in Lebanon today, the Christians were the poorest, but that it did not show because they have a "different lifestyle." He said he could prove that "the Shi`a are the richest Lebanese community, because look at the number of children they have. Anybody who is not rich cannot afford to have 10 children." He talked about the fear of the Christians, especially the Maronites of the Mountain, of the Muslim population, and maintained that the Shi`a have used demography as a weapon in a deliberate effort to become the most numerous sect in Lebanon and take it over, and that they have succeeded.

I told him that I would swear now on any sacred book he wants that should the Shi`a take control of Lebanon, I would convert to Maronitism in order to always be on the side of the minority and defend its rights.

I did not like the Lebanon I saw this morning either.

July 29, 2006

I haven't written anything in a couple of days, and that's because I have become a robot, and robots don't write creative prose. It is also because nothing noteworthy has happened for a couple of days. The past forty-eight hours have been filled with more of the same: Bush and Blair reciting their litany about Israel-the-victim who cannot cease fire, Israel pounding hundreds of villages in Lebanon relentlessly, more dead women and children (someone will have to explain to me one day why the death of civilian adult males is less poignant than that of women and children), more rockets on Israeli settlements and cities, more wimpish Lebanese politicians, more grandiloquent rhetoric by fewer Arab demonstrators, more demonstrations in Europe than in the Arab World, more apologetic Arab leaders begging the US for forgiveness for being of the same nation as Hizbullah and promising that they will never let this happen again, more Hizbullah gutsiness, and more obscure prospects than ever. These are times of plenty. Of the wrong things.

I met a friend yesterday who is working on a documentary on the people of Beirut she is friends with (liberal bourgeois intellectuals). She is asking them, as a family, to talk about the days we are all living. She told me that it was terrible that all the people she had interviewed were against Hizbullah and blamed the war on them, and that they are forgetting that it is Israel and not Hizbullah (short for the Shi`a of Lebanon) who were destroying the country. I agreed that this was awful especially given that a recent poll (which appeared today in the anti-Hizbullah English-language Lebanese newspaper *The Daily Star*, and was carried out by an independent polling institute called the Beirut Center for Research and Information) showed overwhelming support of the Lebanese for Hizbullah. Of course, opinion diverged on sectarian lines, the least supportive being the Druze and the most supportive the Shi`a, but highly controversial actions such as the kidnapping of the soldiers still got 70% support by all those interviewed, while support for Hizbullah's response to the Israelis was close to 90%. Basically, the picture in today's Lebanon is that the rich (who can absorb these events better than anyone and whose main complaint has been that their fun summer has been ruined) are against the Resistance, while the poor (many of whom have already lost everything) are pro-Resistance! How hypocritical and weak is the bourgeoisie when its comfort is at stake!

Sayed Hassan Nasrallah has just addressed the nation to tell the Lebanese not to fear anything and that victory was certain.

Later that night P. came for dinner. He is the head of UNICEF's operations in Water and Sanitation. He is based in New York, but came to Beirut a few days ago to check what could be done in WatSat (water and sanitation). Muna and I had met him in 1991 in Yemen. He was then in Oxfam's technical Unit and Muna was their representative in Yemen, and we had to deal with a large scale refugee crisis when the Saudis expelled hundreds of thousands of poor Yemeni laborers in response to Yemen's political stance in the first Gulf War. P. is a great guy, short and stocky and with white hair and matching beard. He is so full of energy that you are always expecting him to launch into an Irish jig right there and then. P.'s main problem is he talks continuously, something I hate because this is usually my role.

P. is trying to set up a volunteer-based action unit to alleviate the WatSat situation which, in his view, is quickly becoming catastrophic. He asked me if I could help by drafting engineering or environmental sciences students. We agreed we'd give it a shot, but that it would need to be very structured, with clear allocations of duties and reporting lines, as all the work I have been trying to do so far has ended up in a mess. He told us that UNICEF had several million U.S. dollars available, but that it was unable to use them because of the slowness and the bureaucracy of the UN system. He told me they had to wait for clearances from every possible side, but especially from the Israelis, if they were to move a pencil sharpener from the second to the third floor. We bitched about the UN for the rest of the evening, him waxing nostalgic for the times he was at Oxfam, and Muna and I drawing on our experiences of the UNDP, WHO and ESCWA. It must be said that the innate hypocrisy of a system made out of people who earn obscenely large amounts of money for supporting the needy and who disappear suddenly and *en masse* when the needy most need them is just intolerable. That is without pointing at the enslaving of the UN by the U.S. which has no respect whatsoever for this obsolete association of incompetent bureaucrats. I mean look at Kofi Annan. Israel just killed four UN observers in a deliberate bombing. He just stood there with his usual sad, impotent looks wearing his 'Bolton Rules' t-shirt.

July 30, 2006

I waited till the end of this day to write in my journal. I usually purposely delay the daily task of fishing back the memories of my day, at least the most marking of them, from the troubled swamp that is my short-term memory, and then polish them, observe them before laying them on the computer screen. Today I am just afraid of what I have to write.

Last night the Israeli air force destroyed a shelter where more than sixty women, children, and handicapped people had sought refuge in the village of Qana in South Lebanon. They all died, buried under the rubble. I saw on TV their families, their relatives and their friends, those who remained and who looked deader than the deceased, pull them from under the chunks of broken walls and arrange them next to each other, in an infinite line of dusty but intact bodies. If it wasn't for the way they were being carried, held by their limbs as if they were sheep, one could have thought they were sleeping. From time to time, a press photographer or a journalist extended a helpful hand. From time to time, a man would drop his burden, so light in his arms but so heavy in his soul, and collapse in tears. The women were wailing, the men were shouting their anger, and all, all, even the foreign journalists were expressing loudly their indignation of a massacre they knew would remain unpunished. The Chosen People do not pay debts. And they never give IOUs.

In Tel Aviv, Condoleezza Rice, the U.S. Secretary of State, expressed her sadness, but she went on, these are things that happen in wars.

The Israeli prime minister, Ehud Olmert, blamed Hizbullah. To convince us, he constructed a very simple argument: If there was no Hizbullah, Israel wouldn't have needed to bomb Lebanon, and all these innocent deaths could have been avoided. The whole world listened to him. Many people believed him, especially in the West. The black sheep like us knew he was lying, but they were scared of saying anything, so they just moved their heads up and down and sideways so that the world could read in it both negation and acquiescence, and they went baaa baaa.

The families of the victims promised to keep fighting Israel till their last breath.

July 31, 2006

I woke up very early this morning, as I do everyday. I made coffee and switched the TV on. The morning news was full of war and death. There were mostly images of children lying next to each other as if they were peacefully sleeping, eyes wide open. We could tell they were dead because their parents, hysterical with pain, were moving them around to show them to the press photographers without the care usually reserved to the living.

A voice over was informing us that the UN Security Council, which had convened a special session last night, had expressed its profound sadness for the death of the 60 women and children of Qana, buried in their shelter by an Israeli mega bomb. The Security Council had not found it necessary to condemn this attack or to impose an immediate ceasefire, but there were talks of a 24-hours truce to bury the dead.

The job of the palace eunuchs has always been to counsel the monarch and to take care of his dirty work, without ever antagonizing him.

This is when I decided to go to Sinay, my village in the South. I'd had enough of my daily routine and of my self-inflicted isolation. I had to see with own eyes my country and the state in which the enemies put it. I wanted to surprise Suhayla and my other cousins and tell them my love. I had at least ten other perfectly valid reasons when I only needed one: I needed air, emotions, danger. In my house in Beirut I was starting to get moldy.

I took the road on my brother Tarek's bike, a 250cc Kawasaki Ninja, stylish in spite of its small engine. I had barely joined the airport road when a speeding truck flashed its lights and overtook me. It was filled with large badly sealed sacks from which emanated the vilest stench, a smell of carrion macerated in rotten fruits. The vehicle was leaving behind it a trail of solid matter of various sizes that collided with my face, my chest, my helmet, and filled my lungs. When a flattened metal can skimmed my helmet, I understood that this was the solid waste hearse of Beirut delivering its load to the burial grounds of Na`meh.

I exited the highway and waited for a few minutes. I knew this trip would be dangerous, but if I had to die, I would rather it be at the hands of the Israelis.

There were very few people on the Khaldeh road, and traffic thinned further towards Na`meh, which stank of badly buried waste. I was riding fast, easily passing all the cars. It was more interesting to ride than I had thought, and I quickly rediscovered my reflexes. A good thing too, because right after the bend at the entrance to Na`meh, the road was blocked with a mountain of metal scrap and cement blocks. This is all that was left of the bridge that once crossed over the highway. A temporary diversion towards a side road had been opened. I took it and found myself in the center of the village. It was swarming with Lebanese army troops. The shop fronts that had been blown out by the explosions were open, and the activity was surprising. I stayed on the small road till Damour where all the cars took the mountain road. I asked the Lebanese army checkpoint if there was another way. The soldiers told me to rejoin the highway, as I would be able to pass with the bike.

I rode alone for a while on the deserted road. Soon, I saw in the distance a mound of debris similar to the one I had encountered in Na`meh. There were many cars parked around it, and a man seemed to be doing some work in the distance. I went towards him.

The crater must have been 30 meters in diameter. It was partly filled with its own rubble, but I could also see a number of destroyed cars. As to the ones I thought were parked, they were all burned and torn. The man was busy filing one of the sides of the gaping hole with stones and sand, in order to make a passage wide enough for cars to wade through on this river of wreckage. I was able to pass easily and stopped to ask him if the road to Saida was clear.

At this moment, a minivan bursting with women and children arrived from the south. To pass the improvised bridge, they had to step out of the bus and walk to the other side. They were coming from Nabatiyeh where they had spent the last 3 days in a dark and stinky shelter where they had to defecate and urinate on the floor, right in front of each others, like beasts in a stable. They had tried their luck at dawn, and had safely reached Saida where they had waited several hours before finding a driver who had accepted to take them to Beirut in exchange for their last savings. The women stood stoically with their long veils twirling in the breeze. They were looking incredulously at the horizon and the sea, without seeming to understand where they were. They breathed deeply, to fill their lungs with the smell of seaweed, thyme and the perfumes of the land as if to eliminate the dirty air of the shelter. The children were catatonic, their heads filled with sleep and with images of noisy death. The families had no idea where to go after reaching Beirut.

I took the old coastal road, as I was told. There were columns of smoke in the distance. I knew it was the Jiyyeh power plant, where the fuel tanks had been burning for over15 days. I reached Sa`adiyat, where my uncle Ziad had taught me how to gather sea urchins way before the wars started. There wasn't a single car in sight, and I was in Jiyyeh very quickly. This is where the 'hottest' beaches of Lebanon are located. They have evocative names : Janna,

Pangea, Jonas, Bamboo Bay. Luxurious places where the customers are carefully filtered at the entrance. I remembered that I had promised myself never to set foot there again. Five or six years ago, my family and that of my friend Tuha had decided to spend the day at the beach. We went to the place called Jonas. The fat man at the gate wanted to take our names in order to book a beach umbrella and I answered him in Arabic. I gave my name as well as Tuha's, which in reality is Abdul-Fattah Amhaz: you can't get more Shi`a than that. The man looked at me as if he was regretting to have told us that there were vacancies. He then said: "you know this is a classy beach, you can't grill meat or prepare a narguileh." To this day, I feel pain in the stomach and in the nape of my neck when I think about the incident. I know I should have broken his teeth and gone home instead of following my wife's advice and avoid spoiling the day. But that was a long time ago when I was young and stupid and without rancor.

The stench of burning fuel was infernal, and the carcinogenic cloud had spread over more than a kilometer. I crossed it literally blindly. When I exited this Gahanna, the sea in Rmeileh was turquoise, and the waves were languorously dying on the black sticky sand.

The great bridge at the entrance to Saida had disappeared. All that remained were two powerless stumps trying in vain to grasp each other. I took the small road towards the temple of Eshmun, the Phoenician War God. The smell of orange blossoms impregnated the humid and motionless air. Suddenly there was nothing other than this palpable smell that seemed to emanate from the pores of the earth, from the wood of the trees and from the leafy shadows. It intoxicated me and I dissolved myself in it, thinking about death.

At the Saida exit, there were Lebanese army soldiers, slouching at the tables in front of a *mana'ish* bakery. I made the mistake of asking them if the highway was open. They immediately became suspicious and asked me for my identity papers. I obeyed while remarking sarcastically about the absurdity of their request and about the imbecility of an Israeli spy who would stop to ask directions from the army. They told me to take the old road and to watch out for the Israeli helicopters that were hunting Resistance bikers riding on the southern roads.

The traffic on the road to Sour was moving pretty well and could have almost been 'normal', if it weren't for the absence of trucks, which were also being specifically hunted by the enemy air force. The passing cars were carrying whole families with mattresses and blankets on the roof. They all had white flags hanging from the windows or tied to the radio antennas.

I reached Ghazieh, which had been bombed several times. In front of the restaurants-butcheries aligned on the main road, men were lighting up large barbecues. The smell of the grilled meat stopped me for a minute and took me back a few months, to a lunch stop we made, a friend and I, on our way back from Sinay. I didn't stay long. There is nothing worse than the stench of cold barbecue, the sickening stench of which sticks to the hair and to the clothes, and which can only be eliminated with a complete scrubbing.

A few kilometers later, I left the coastal road and rode towards the ochre hills of the Jabal `Amel in its summer attire.

The narrow and sinuous road that links my village to the coast passes by Bissariyeh, Ghassaniyeh, Kawtarieh, then through the isolated valley of Khartoum. There wasn't any traffic; I had fun carving the bends. The bike was well balanced, and its handling excellent. I would have liked it to have more power, but it was good enough, and it almost made me forget the danger of driving on this road, where the 'Apache' helicopters could appear at any time. Lost in my thoughts, I realized the absurdity of being shot by a war machine to which the Americans had given the name of one of the tribes they had exterminated. When it comes to money, the Americans are capable of doing anything, even of recycling the glory of their victims. Will the next generation of U.S. planes be called 'Hizbullah'?

A few minutes later, I passed the large flamboyant bougainvillea hedge and took the small road to Sinay. Suddenly I was in my cousin's old house. We kissed without letting anyone see us, because it is not done in the village, then we cried together for her daughter who had died two months before. We drank the very dark and very sweet tea we make in my region. Sitting on the couch, I let peace penetrate me while my cousins talked about the war.

August 1, 2006

I'm back in Beirut. It's a bad day for me for no reasons except the obvious ones. I think depression is starting to show. Maybe it's because I've started seeing people, friends of Muna, who are doctors at AUB and who work with her in the volunteer unit. They're really nice and we share a lot politically, but somehow this is depressing me. Maybe because we only talk about one thing: the holocaust about to happen, compared to which all that has been going on in the past three weeks is kid's stuff.

I have lost all feeling, as well as the capacity to love, to be affectionate and to look forward to a beautiful, happy life. But every night I have dreams of tenderness and love and happiness which all end abruptly in the morning. I go to sleep every night looking for them.

In Lebanon at war, no wonder I'm starved for tenderness and simple happiness. But when I am awake, I know this does not exist, that war is a fact of life, like getting grey hair, arthritis, wrinkles, and poor eyesight.

August 2, 2006

I'm running late on everything today. It's weird to say that, as we are under siege and I'm not doing much, but this is exactly how I feel. It's like I have a job (my 'routine') and I have to go through all the motions otherwise my life will collapse. This is how bad it is: A couple of days ago, Muna and I decided to leave home early and go queue for petrol, which is becoming increasingly rare, but not the cars. (There is was a traffic jam in Hamra this morning, how come?). We were at the station at 6:30 AM and there were already over a hundred cars waiting. I convinced Muna that we had enough petrol (we must have around a hundred liters between my car, the van, Muna's car, the truck, and her sister's car: enough to go to Turkey and come back). We were back home at seven. I couldn't go running after that, although I often leave home much later than that. It was as if my whole schedule had been messed up, and because I had introduced a new element into it, I could not go through all the other steps.

I guess it is a normal reaction to the idleness and the depression imposed on us by the war. I must have created these 'important' tasks which are not to be messed with in order to convince myself that my life is still 'normal' and that I'm not just sitting here, waiting to learn where the Israelis have just bombed, or trying to guess where they will bomb next. We each hang onto our sanity in our own way.

This war is very different from the last big one I was in, the Israeli invasion of 1982. I had stayed in Beirut then too, and there was very little of everything for everyone. This time, if you are in Ras Beirut, it is as if you were in Austria. Admittedly, there are no deer in the AUB forest, but everything else is available for those who have been spared the destruction and who continue to earn a living even if they do nothing. This includes me. Should one want to, one could go to the beach everyday, have drinks in pubs, and go out with friends. In Broummana and other areas, it is as if there was no war. Friends who have moved there tell me they have big parties till dawn, which they end watching the fireworks: the Israeli bombing of the Southern suburbs. This, at least, is reminiscent of the 1982 war, when the people of East Beirut got drunk and smoked dope watching the daily bombardments of the city where I lived.

In Beirut today, everything is available, fruits, vegetables, bread, meat, there is even a sushi place advertising itself as being open. On my way from the South the other day, I saw many trucks filled with vegetables going towards Beirut. People have to make a living and they take risks for selling aubergines to the rich.

These are the small things of my life these days. I just heard that Hizbullah had hit the military operations center in Israel, and that Israel said it would retaliate by bombing Beirut. What will tomorrow bring?

August 3, 2006

I'm not listening to any music these days. My iPod has been silent almost since the beginning of the war. I'm not in a cheerful mood. I'm not in an English or French mood. I'm not in a love mood. Sometimes I enjoy leftist revolutionary songs from the 70s but they remind me too much of when we still believed in international struggle and in the power of the people and were hopeful. Today we are fighting and we know we will win, but we know there is no hope to change the world in our life time. That's why I'm not in a mood for music or for cheering our military achievements and our human misery. I'm not sure how I'll come out of this war, whichever way it ends. I feel today that I am so divorced from the rest of Lebanon, from the rest of the world. The only places that make any sense to me are West Beirut, the Southern Suburbs, and the South. I don't think I will be able to go anywhere else in a long time. I don't think I'll be able to join the happy mezze eating of the Lebanese, or the oh-so-affected natural cuisine and lifestyle of Souk el Tayyeb. I just want to go hide in the South, and be with my people, my family, my blood, and my life. Friends have been inviting us to visit them in places in the 'Christian' areas like Broummana, Jbeil, Batroun. I'm not even answering their phones, I don't want to make excuses and I don't want to hurt them by telling them the truth.

My village is starting to get hit. I've called and they're doing fine, at least those who are still there. I wish I could have stayed there. This is the price of having a family. I feel I need to split my skin and get out of it, renewed, like the animals that shed their skins. I want to be with my people under the bombs.

August 5, 2006

It was a heavy night. I was woken around 2:00 AM by the ceaseless circling of the Israeli war planes, passing and passing again very low over the buildings, scaring the hell out of everything alive. And with every passage, you think: this is the one; this is when they will bomb. But then they pass, and the glass panes rattle. It gets to the absurd points where you start wishing them to bomb and get it over with, anything is better than this tension. Of course, it is not true. I mean, being bombed is not better than being scared from imminent bombing, but you only know that after they bomb. This happened around 4:00 AM. The house started shaking; the kids woke up in terror and flocked to our bed. I left the bed to them and Muna, made coffee and switched the TV on. There was electricity, and that was a small blessing in the middle of this huge curse. The camera of New TV was aimed at a huge column of smoke billowing in the morning dimness. It must have been installed on one of the hills overlooking the city and it kept moving right and left, from Ouzai to the southern suburbs. I could hear the deafening sounds of the bombs, and see immediately on TV the smoke coming out of the location that was hit. It would have been impressive had it not meant more death, pain, loss and displacement. The line between genuine journalism and macabre voyeurism must be really thin.

Around 6 AM, the sound of the bombing started to reach me from the opposite side and the New TV camera did not show anything new. I switched channels, and found out that the highway bridges between Jounieh, Jbeil, and Batroun were being targeted. They pounded them repeatedly till about 7:00 AM. Now Beirut was cut off the rest of Lebanon from all directions except from the East, the Syrian side.

But Beirut itself was not hit.

This intensification in the level of bombing, and the targeting of areas in the Christian side of the country came as a response to last night's speech by Hassan Nasrallah. This is a speech that will enter history. Not because it was of particularly good literary quality, but because of what he said, and how he said it. Imagine that, a speech by an Arab contemporary leader that is as important in content as in form! That alone would make it memorable.

Nasrallah covered many points in his speech, but one was especially relevant to this morning's shelling: The Israelis had declared yesterday that they were now moving to hit Lebanon "in its depth, including Beirut." He, very calmly, said: "Well, you already are bombing Lebanon in its depth, and all people of Lebanon are equal, but Beirut is our capital, and if you bomb our capital, we will bomb yours. Capital for capital, Tel Aviv for Beirut. I promised there will be Haifa, and so it was. I promised there will be beyond Haifa, and so it was. And I promised beyond beyond Haifa, and it will be."

The rest of the speech was bold, very calmly declaimed, with none of the political haranguing common to Arab leaders. He addressed Arab heads of state and told them that their thrones will not be thrones in the US-designed New Middle East. He paved the way to a ceasefire by promising to stop the rockets if the Israelis stop their air raids. He briefed the world about the state of the front lines, and, unlike other Arab leaders, the people believe him. Even those who do not like him. Especially those who do not like him.

We may all die in this war. We may all want to die in this war. But I am happy that before my death I will have heard a speech by an Arab leader that was good to listen to, that was not filled with empty rhetoric and no action, but that had been written on the basis of achievements in the field of action. A speech that was not a cover-up filled with lies. It's a pity my kids were not old enough to understand it, because they will regret it later.

Now, Israel doesn't take standing up to it very well, so each time he does that, they go nuts and start bombing furiously. I must say that he was very personal with Olmert, and told him that he had a grandeur complex and that he matched Sharon's savagery but not his political skills.

After the morning bombing, things got quieter and I went to run errands: bank, electricity, and food. On my way I met an old friend, E., who is a reporter for many francophone magazines. We came home for coffee and we got talking about the war, Israel, the Shi`a, and Hizbullah. She wanted my take on the war and I said that I fully supported the Resistance. She said that she did too, but that they should let her do her job more freely. She had been everywhere, Bint Jbeil, Sur, Qana, and had seen everything. She said the worse were not the corpses, but the survivors coming out of the rubble. She told me she had witnessed an attack by an Israeli helicopter on a minivan loaded with refugees, and that after hitting the minivan and killing many of the passengers, the helicopter had chased the survivors into the fields and shot them one by one. They were all women and children. When she wrote the story for her Belgian magazine, the editor called and said: "That was a very interesting story, very moving, but somewhere else you say that the Israelis are carrying out pin-point accuracy raids, so how come you say they shot the minivan?" She tried to explain that shooting fleeing civilians was pin-point accuracy, but that the idea would not permeate his skull thickened by years of Israeli propaganda.

She too could not believe that I shared views and opinions with the people of the Resistance and with Hizbullah. She asked me what my driving force was, and I said that for the time being, I recognized Hassan Nasrallah as a great leader, but that my support to Hizbullah is limited to its opposition to Israel and to its commitment to armed struggle. I told her that Israel was a terrorist state, and that it has never hesitated to resort to force, and that the Arabs are scared because they are cowards and have lost their pride. And that I am a believer in the rights of people all people to a decent life and to pride. And that pride is a basic human right, not a luxury only accessible to some people. And that Israel is a state that was born from violence, and that it was built on forcefully robbing the Palestinians of their homes, their lands and their rights, with the complicity of the Great Nations and of the UN. And therefore there was nothing to expect from these nations.

I also told her that we have an ethical and moral duty to oppose Zionism as a doctrine that is racist and that cultivates oppression. And I wonder, I said, why you the French do not understand that. This is the same debate that shook France in the 1930s when Fascism started to gain strength. The Spanish civil war was the object of lengthy discussions and the leftist government of France refused to support the leftists in Spain. Some went to fight and became the International Brigade, the stuff of legends. But throughout the war, the French leftist government refused to give its support to the Spanish freedom fighters, while Italy and Germany were both arming the fascists. The results were horrifying, and Guernica stands witness to your crocodile tears. The Picasso painting of the women and children being bombed in Qana—pardon Guernica—is now a priceless work of art. But do you remember that you made Guernica possible, because the French left decided to be pragmatic and to abandon the Spanish left to its fate? This is similar to the pragmatism preached nowadays by the Lebanese government and other political parties and by the Arab governments. I call it defeatism and fear of losing one's comfort by standing for a belief. Many massacres took place in Spain as the fascist army bombed the insurgents with Mussolini's planes. Rings a bell? Eventually, the fascists ruled Spain for many decades, and you deplore that to this day, conveniently forgetting that you made it happen.

Then she raised the issue that not all the Lebanese want to 'resist' and among those who do, many do not wish to engage in armed struggle. Moreover, she said, the association of the Resistance with Syria and Iran was not acceptable to many as these are dictatorial undemocratic and murderous regimes. I told her that this is also a debate that went on in France, both before and after its invasion by the Nazis. There was a camp of peace-loving intellectuals, like the philosopher Alain, who wanted to preserve peace at any cost, and who believed that it was possible to reach a *modus vivendi* with the fascists in Europe, and that the Nazis were calling for negotiations and friendly relations within a 'Great Europe'. Others were adamant that armed struggle was the only possible way to put an end to these regimes because their very existence was a threat to humanity. The communists were all over the place, with the war at first and then against it when Stalin signed a pact with Hitler. History proved those who did not trust Hitler to be right. When the Nazis invaded France, the Resistance was not appreciated by all, and the French government of Vichy, headed by Pierre Laval, was coerced in the name of 'pragmatism' to work forcefully to end the armed resistance. Vichy France made friends with the Nazis, and hundreds of thousands of Jews and communists were deported from France and ended in Dachau and Treblinka. The Resistance forged an alliance with the British, a country that was France's sworn enemy for centuries, and that is how they won the war. And please, do not tell me that Britain was a more 'humane' and 'democratic' regime than Syria or Iran. This is the Britain of the British Raj, the most imperialist nation in modern history (they have been beaten by the U.S. now, and guess who the U.S. supports? That's right, not us). Britain massacred hundreds of thousands of indigenous people and destroyed nations and countries to establish its rule over the world and plunder its resources. And we are bad because Syria and Iran support us? They are, as we say in Arabic, a drop in the sea compared to the U.S. (of the Native Americans fame), Britain (of the Raj and Africa fame) and France (remember, North Africa, Equatorial Africa?). No, we take moral lessons from no one.

We talked about the Shi`a psyche, and I discovered that all she knew about us could fit into one small paragraph. She had been a journalist in Lebanon for nearly seven years, covering the wars and ignoring who the Shi`a were, and what Jabal `Amel was. And she said she was by far the most erudite of the bunch she works with, including her Lebanese colleagues at *L'Orient-Le Jour*. In fact, especially her Lebanese colleagues.

During our discussion, I made a frightening discovery. We were talking about the famous sentence by Robert Fisk in his July 17 article in *The Independent*, where he makes an argument for stopping the war because: "*They look like us, the people of Beirut. They have light-coloured skin and speak beautiful English and French. They travel the world. Their women are gorgeous and their food exquisite*" (emphasis added). She justified Fisk by saying that unless the most limited, poorly-educated, western readers can identify with the victim, they will not feel empathy and will not lift a finger, (and will not read the article and therefore buy the paper). This is why she, like all reporters writing for the foreign press, must paint a picture of the Lebanese as being almost white and 'civilized'. I said that this is the epitome of despair: That in order for the Westerners to recognize our plea and sufferings, we must lose our identity and agree to be 'swallowed' by a different culture. To have their support, we must look like them, talk like them, eat like them, fuck like them, in short, be a poor imitation of them. So the choice is either be monkeys (which we Lebanese are pretty good at) and earn empathy, or die nameless in total indifference. As she put it: "I'm sorry, I hate it, but that's how it is. You have to face it. The West runs the world, and you are just items in the news. If you want them to identify with you and support you, then we must present you as if you were like them. You have no choice."

I said of course we have a choice; we have the choice of dying free, and not giving a shit about what the West thinks. They can only enslave us because they can take our lives, but when we do not care about our lives, then we are free. They can take our lives, but they cannot take our death. And before we die, we will take a lot of them with us, and grin at them forever in the afterlife.

August 5, 2006

A very old friend from the days of the 1975 war and who lives in the southern suburbs came to see me last night. We kept talking till late in the night. It was unbelievably saddening and I was very happy to see him. Go figure. What I make from our conversation is that there is absolutely and categorically no future for Lebanon as we knew it. The country has always been polarized, but this time this is not a political polarization, it is a survival polarization. Each party knows that there can only be one winner to this war, and that the loser will have to forfeit all claims to Lebanon for the next generation. On one side you have the March 14th forces. On the other the Resistance force and the Aounis. The March 14th agenda fits well with the US/Israeli plans for the region, while the Hizbullah (with Aoun so far) agenda aligns with the Iranian agenda. The Syrians are in between like vultures, waiting till the last moment to hedge their bets.

This is the situation. If Hizbullah wins, they will dominate the Muslim political scene and the Aounis the Christian scene. If the other side wins, the Future Movement and the Lebanese forces and consort will dominate. I have also learned today that in the Palestinian camps, the Fatah people are being groomed by Hariri to fight on the side of the Sunni should the war deteriorate into a Sunni-Shi'a conflict like Iraq. There are 6,000 armed men in the camps, and the head of Fatah in Lebanon, Sultan Abu al`Ainein, went from being wanted by the Lebanese police for terrorist activity to being received in the Hariri palace and at the Maronite Patriarch in Bkerkeh as an official diplomat. He was declared innocent without trial.

What a mess. All of this means is that it isn't over yet.

Muna and I went for a walk in Hamra last night. We took a stroll on Makdessi Street and there were few shops open, but there were many people in the streets, all refugees from the South and the suburbs. They were sitting on the streets near the buildings where they have found shelter, and some, especially the women, were buying food and vegetables from the shops that were still open. The kids were everywhere, tens of them. The men were blocking the sidewalk smoking narguileh. They all looked content which is admirable considering the fact that they are homeless and that most may have lost all their possessions and have sons fighting in the south. Then we got to the Café de Prague, which is on the same street. It was like passing into a different country. Young people drinking beer, courting, discussing, smoking, and eating bar food. So uncanny, so bizarre.

We saw an old friend inside Prague so we stepped in to say hi. When he saw me, he made a poor imitation of the Southern accent and asked me ironically if I was fighting. He is a nice guy and means no harm so I gave him the grin I have developed over thirty-five years of hearing sarcasm about the Shi`a by people who think that my being born into a Shi`a family was accidental. He invited us for a drink and I declined politely.

We took Hamra Street on our way back, and it was like the Southern Suburbs overlaid onto Hamra Street. There were girls in spaghetti straps side by side with nun-like hijabed girls with or without chaperones. There were groups of young men, in casual clothing and gelled hair, following the girls from a distance, and stopping now and then for ice cream or a cold drink. We stopped for a juice, and people thought I was a foreigner (my shorts and t-shirt and white hair and Muna's red hair) and kept addressing me in English. I kept answering in Arabic, but they just marveled at my ability to speak the local language and continued talking to me in broken English. I used to get that a lot in Yemen, but in Lebanon it's a first. Everybody seemed to be having a good time, and the atmosphere (although it was crowded and God knows I hate crowds) was peaceful.

We passed by the windows of Lina's cafe and it was like watching a documentary on the habits and behavior of a different social class on TV.

August 7, 2006

It's been a tough night or rather early morning, as we were woken by repeated air strikes. Yesterday they flattened a house in Ansar, which is less than a kilometer away from my house in Sinay. There were six dead: one sleeping family goes away. This dawn, they did the same in the village of Ghassaniyeh, right next door to Sinay, on the road to Saida: another family of six disappeared. I am told Sinay is now almost empty as people have joined the ranks of the refugees. One million people on the streets.

I'm sick of talking about the war, thinking about the war, breathing the war, drinking, and eating the war. I feel now that I don't know anything else anymore, and that if it stopped I wouldn't know what to do. I think I'm never going to be in a good mood ever again.

August 8, 2006

I've just had a long conversation with a friend who came seeking intellectual solace. She is Palestinian and is fully committed to the Resistance. She needed to talk to someone who shares her political views so that we can be mutually reinforcing. We had a very long discussion about the present, the prospects, our actions and activities and how are we supporting and helping people around us, how this war as changed us and what we expect from it. We also vented off a lot about how we believe the West and the rest of the world perceives us, and how this affects us and how this war is different from all others. There are a couple of issues that stood out.

One of these is the fact that Israel is capable of acting with impunity with the approval of the whole world, as is shown by the international opinion polls and the relatively small number of people participating in anti-war demonstrations worldwide. I know it's a well known fact but I can't help it, I find it infuriating and when I think of it I just want to beat my chest very hard and shout very loudly. Two days ago, Israel kidnapped the head of the Palestinian legislative council in the West Bank, jailed him and beat him till he needed hospitalization. This is a democratically elected leader in Palestine. What did the world say? Nothing. Israel and the US have launched an unprecedented war on Lebanon to 'rid it of Hizbullah.' Most targets are civilians; most of the dead are women and children. Their pictures have been shown to the whole world. Last night, a whole building in a heavily populated area of Beirut, near

Tayyouneh, was destroyed. There are at least forty dead and one hundred wounded. Who cares? Only a few. We used to be able to count on the international left, not anymore. Why?

The answer is simple. In previous wars, we hid behind Arabism, revolutionarism and leftism and barely ever mentioned Islam. Across the globe, pro-Arabs, revolutionaries and leftists were ready to take our side and to request an end to violence against us. Today, in Lebanon, the people doing the fighting cannot be camouflaged under another label. They are plain Muslims, and, more importantly, Muslims who refuse to submit to the Empire. They look ugly to the Westernized eye, dress differently, speak English very poorly, and well, they are just 'not like us' (see Fisk's comment about the Lebanese earlier). The Western media has made it its job to demonize them and present them as the antithesis to Rationalism and to Reason. Regular, liberal well-meaning Westerners cannot see themselves as supporters of Muslim 'fundamentalists' who are burly, dress weirdly and represent the Saracen, the Moor, the infidel. Look at Nasrallah. How different he must look to the Westerners. And, given the constant hammering by the media against mullahs and Islam, how can they ever get to accept him as a freedom fighter?

As for the Western right-wingers, I will not even talk about these. If they're ever on our side, it's only for anti-Semitic reasons and we should reject their support. It is the Left that has been giving me most trouble. I have really good Western friends who have been very supportive of the Arabs over the past twenty years and who have suddenly, in this war, become Israeli apologists. I was stunned. But then it came to me: they'd rather have Israel kill us all than have Muslims win the battle. They hide behind their secularism, but in reality, it is the same visceral dislike for Muslims who are Muslims and who declare themselves Muslims and who have made this war a Muslim war. By the way, this analysis applies also to those among the Lebanese who'd rather see their country ruled by Israel and the US rather than have Hizbullah which, unlike the Amal movement, is unequivocally a religious party, gain influence and strength in Lebanon.

I do not want to be under Islamic rule, and I disagree with the social agenda and with large chunks of their political agenda of Hizbullah, but *certainly* I will never ever support Israel. This is because of a matter of ethics and morals, and because Israel (and the U.S.) are colonizing nations which have both been built on the oppression and robbery of the lands of weaker people who had never done them any harm. Israel and the U.S. (and much of the West) continue to support themselves through racist and terrorist policies and through terrorizing nations into submission. Basically the choices today are simple: we either submit or we are killed. No third way. I don't see Hizbullah submitting any time soon, if anything because they know the thumbs of the U.S. Caesars will be pointing down when they do. There is no mercy to be expected.

I really think the most likely scenario is one of a Lebanese implosion. Hizbullah may be winning on the military scene, but this is not very important as the two-pronged and highly synchronized attack of the U.S. politicians (I disregard other politicians on purpose, they don't exist in this war) and the Israeli army is working well: destroy a country and kill as many civilians as you can to prepare the grounds for an unconditional surrender by Hizbullah. The political battle is being fought in New York. The seven points of the ceasefire requested by the Lebanese government give more concessions to the Israelis than resolution 1559, and the U.S. won't even agree to that! The U.S. are fighting a win-win war, it is not their soldiers who are dying, and they don't care about the Lebanese people, civilians or not, Christians or Muslims or Hindus. Now go convince Hizbullah that they will be left in peace in a U.S.-dominated Lebanon. The Americans will take them all to Guantanamo, after finding them guilty of killing Hariri, Kennedy, and the Archduke Ferdinand.

That is why I do not see an end to this war any time soon.

An ex-good friend (I have become very picky about my friendships recently) once said to me: "The Shi`a want everything quickly and by force. I do not agree with this way of doing things. You have to integrate into Lebanon and work your way up through education instead of crying your misfortune and claiming that you are discriminated against when you are merely poorly educated." She is herself Shi`a.

I realized what was bothering me with this argument. I may agree with the merit-based approach given equal chances; and with knowledge as an essential component of development. But in reality, the Shi`a (and others) are not accepted or rejected on the basis of their level of knowledge. The discrimination is on the basis of culture. This is what she meant by "education." It is not enough to be up to standards in science, technology, know-how, business. You also have to look the part. And if you look the part, meaning you look foreign and you speak excellent English and preferably French and you are culturally Western, then this is more important than your diplomas and your knowledge and you are preferentially selected. Take a Shi`a woman in hijab or chador. Place her among the crowd in Saatchi and Saatchi's office or in a similar environment. Don't go that far; let them try to find a job as a schoolteacher in a fancy school, or even to be a waiter in a restaurant downtown. Do you think that whatever their skills they will get the job? No way! To do that, they might need to have skills, to be versed in technology, to possess modern knowledge, *but* more importantly, they will have to give up who they are and become western clones.

This war has amply demonstrated that the Shi'a do not have a genetic aversion for technology, knowledge, and learning and that they can access it and use it much better than many who look the part. I'm sure they did not hit the Israeli ship with two rockets by aiming in the general direction and reading the appropriate Quranic verse. I'm sure that if Manar TV station is still broadcasting after hundred of air raids it is not because it is protected by the Imam Ali. There is hard-core technology at work here, at a level that is much higher than what most Lebanese have ever been able to comprehend, access and control.

My friend who lives in the southern suburb of Chiyah has not left yet and he has been waiting with his parents, his disabled sister, his wife and five children, for the Israelis to bomb his street. Two nights ago, he took them all and they went to sleep on the sidewalk of the nuns' school his children go to, in Ain el Remaneh. Can you imagine the kids' trauma? You go to the school like the other kids, but everyday you pass by the sidewalk where you and your parents have slept. They left at 5:30 am so that no one would see them, and the moment they got home, the Israelis brought down two buildings two hundred meters away from his house. More trauma. I gave him my camper van and he came last night to sleep on the corniche, near AUB, as the Israelis won't ever bomb an American institution. They had barely left Chiyah when the Israelis raided a building fifty meters away from theirs. Forty dead, hundred wounded at least. When I opened the roof of the camper his twelve-year old daughter started shouting and crying: "Close it, please close it, they will think it's a rocket launcher and kill us all!" It took me a while to understand what she meant.

August 10, 2006

This has been a different day. I went to look for a motorcycle this morning. I need to get around on little petrol. I went with my brother to Dekwaneh, on the eastern side of town, and it felt like being in a different country. For one, the lines on the gas stations are much shorter. People there wait only for three to four hours to get gasoline while people in West Beirut often wait overnight. The traffic jams were also much worse, and the people seemed to be very removed from the war, as if all this was happening in a neighboring country, and there were unavoidable repercussions on them. On my way, I was showered on the Cola intersection by a cloud of Israeli leaflets calling the people of Beirut to wake up to the reality of Hizbullah and of the ruthless and irresponsible Hassan. Not Hassan Nasrallah, just Hassan. What more recognition could they give him? I think they avoid using the name Nasrallah—which means "the Glory of God"—as if that would truly make him the Glory of God. These guys are such primitive Orientalists, I do not know whether to cry or laugh. I'll do both.

My colleague S. who is working in relief called me with a good idea, distributing fresh fruits and vegetables to the displaced to complement their diet. It would cover some of their fiber and vitamins requirements, and help an ailing sector, agriculture, as the export routes are closed. We ranted for an hour or so on the inadequacy and hypocrisy of the UN system, especially that all the bureaucrats are now being relocated to the country of their choice, receiving full salaries plus a per-diem to cover their expenses. This has effectively tripled the salaries of some of them, who never did any useful work anyway and who are not going to start doing any work now.

But the most infuriating thing is the fact that the UN is supposed to be spending its money to help the poor. So to do that better, they leave the countries of the poor and go to the countries of the rich, get overpaid to help the poor from a distance with their fake programs which do not convince anyone anymore. Look at those who left in the first week of the war. Since the UN gave Palestine to the Zionists in the partition plan of 1947, this institution has accumulated a history of unfairness and obedience, nay subservience, to the U.S. I mean Kofi didn't even condemn the deliberate killing of UN troops by the Israelis. What more do you want?

But tomorrow I will start organizing the distribution of fresh fruits and vegetables. Friday will be our launch day, one school, twenty-five families. I hope to be able to cover five hundred families a week. We will need money, but I will get it.

I watched Nasrallah's speech on TV. Very conciliatory, but I think he is calling their bluff by accepting the Lebanese army in the south. I think he knows that will not be enough for the U.S. But now, he has turned the tables, and he is in the 'good guy' position on the Lebanese street. I doubt this will end without a big bang, but I'd love to be proven wrong before fall.

There were seventy dead and twice that many wounded in the Chiyah bombing when the Israeli planes flattened a neighborhood where people were spending a nice summer night outdoors. Most were refugees from other locations in Lebanon. Why didn't anyone talk about a massacre?

Yesterday I paid a visit to my mum's aunt Inaam. She lives in poverty in the huge ancestral house built by my mum's grandfather in the area of Karm el Zaitoun, in Mazraa. Khaled, her nephew lives there too with his family, and my brother Tarek recently lived on the ground floor, which my mum inherited, for over a year. This is a very popular and populated neighborhood, but I have spent there some of the nicest days of my life. I was born there in 1958, during the first post-independence civil war. My father was in Libya then, training their sports teachers and my mother was staying there with her mum. I still bear great attachment to the house where I lost my foreskin. I was circumcised there a few months after my birth by an ambulatory circumciser, as was the custom then. I'm not saying more about it because I don't remember much.

Mazraa is Arabic for farm, and Karm el Zaitoun means "The Olive Grove." At the turn of the twentieth century, this was still a village on the outskirts of Beirut, and the houses were all surrounded with huge fields. It must be around that time that the house of my grandparents was built, a three-story sandstone edifice in the most classical late Ottoman style, with Arabesque tiles and colored glass panes. There used to be a little pool with a water fountain in the center of the tiny garden, and goldfish which I used to bait with a piece of bread on a curved pin held by a sewing thread. There was also an enormous grape vine that climbed all the way from the ground floor to cover the roof of the third floor. We used to sit there at the end of summer, the tallest house in the neighborhood, and eat the small sweet white grapes, shoot with the air rifle and look into the rooms of the adjacent homes hoping to catch a glimpse of a woman, any woman.

I fell in love many times on this street.

My visit to Inaam was something of a pilgrimage. In 1975, I went to live with her as being with my parents was too smothering, and I could not move freely enough to learn about life. During the 1982 invasion and siege of Beirut, Muna and I were still dating, and we used to go on my motorbike (there was very little petrol those days, too) and have a frugal lunch of fried eggplants and potatoes. We were caught there one day by heavy bombing by the Israelis and had to hide in the most protected corner of the house for many hours. This was before today's air raids which can bring down a whole house in a matter of seconds. There is no point hiding now, might as well stay on the top floors, at least your body will be found before it rots.

I was surprised to see my mum's cousin Suzanne there. She is Khaled's sister and the family pariah as she married (as a second wife) the Kurdish driver who used to take her to school, almost twenty-five years ago. It was a real scandal as he was also a devout Sunni Muslim and followed the Ahbash teachings. She was shunned by her family for a long time, and I'm not even sure she has been reinstated as a full-fledged daughter. She was wearing a hijab and looked like my late grand mum, whose long upturned nose she inherited. I asked her if she shook hands with men, but she was quicker and she held me in a very brotherly embrace and kissed me. She smelled like my grandma too. We spoke about the past (I had not seen her in nearly twenty years), and she asked me about Muna and the kids in a mixture of Arabic and French, as if she wanted to show me that she was still the educated young girl with whom I had spent part of my childhood.

August 11, 2006

Tomorrow is the launching date of the Fruits and Vegetables Initiative. I will start it using the logistics of Healthy Basket, the AUB organic Community Supported Agriculture program I founded and with two thousand dollars of seed money I raised from the sister of a Jordanian friend.

Around eleven this morning, while I was still meeting with R. who works in Healthy Basket, there were two very loud explosions. It turned out that an Apache helicopter had launched rockets on the old light-house near the Collège Protestant near the house of Hariri. I think they're trying to get Hizbullah to retaliate in Tel Aviv so they have an excuse to flatten Beirut. They threw more leaflets today asking the people of Burj el Barajneh, Chiyah and Hayy el Sellom to evacuate as they intend to bomb these areas. This is easily quarter of a million people. I think most have left anyway.

August 12, 2006

It's been a couple days since I have written anything significant. In fact since the day Fruits and Vegetables Initiative (FVI) as been launched and I started to do something instead of just ruminating my fate. So first the FVI: It was set up so easily. We just replaced the organic with non-organic in Healthy Basket's well-oiled operations. Hassan (our driver) gets the produce from the wholesale market, and we pack the bags very quickly (about one hundred an hour if we are three). We then call the people in charge of the centers we intend to visit and then drive there. By ten, we've made several hundred people happy. The cost: fifty cents per child per week. We give them tomatoes, cucumbers, carrots (for the beta-carotene), apples and melon. All of these are in season. I'm using the money from a donation that was sent to me and we're trying to locate more funds.

The other *big* thing that has happened is the Security Council resolution which was unanimously passed and which has been endorsed by Lebanon and will be endorsed by Israel tomorrow. It is one of the most unfair UN resolutions I have ever seen. Asa'ad Abu Khalil posted a scathing critique on his blog, Angry Arab. I agree with him that Hizbullah should have never accepted it, but I knew pragmatically that they would. Nasrallah was just on TV to justify their decision. In any case, I think this resolution is the beginning of a new phase for Lebanon and not the end. I still do not see Hizbullah giving up its weapons so easily; they'd be turkeys to do that. In any case, there will be no ceasefire till Monday, and the Israelis are desperately trying to make some headway towards the Litani river, and the resistance fighters are hurting them very hard. There have been at least two important outcomes to this war: 1. The myth of the invincible Israeli army has been destroyed, and we now know that mastery of the air and remote controlled wars do not necessarily succeed; 2. The Shi`a are now in a stronger political position than they've ever been. They have demonstrated that, unlike the other confessional tribes of Lebanon, they have a united political leadership strengthened by a fierce military leadership and supported by a resilient population ready to accept any sacrifice and to tolerate any level of hardship: destruction of houses, massacres, displacement. Nearly a million people were subjected to this treatment with hardly any complaint except against Israel.

The future of this ill-fitting assemblage of tribes that is Lebanon is bound to be strongly affected by these facts. I hope the Shi`a leadership will know how to use it constructively. But more than anything else, I hope the other tribes will know how to deal with this reality. Otherwise, it is doomsday Iraq style.

August 13, 2006

So there it is. The much awaited UNSC resolution 1701 has been passed by all parties, including Hizbullah. I do not feel I am in a position to fully comprehend Hizbullah's ulterior motives to justify accepting such an unjust resolution. I think I have a pretty good idea of what the rationalizations are but I'll come back to that later. I want to have a quick look at the popular/youth Lebanese scene on what is probably the last day of this war as the ceasefire is expected to be implemented tomorrow at 7 AM.

A few days ago, some lawyer whose name has been associated with some of the neocon liberal Lebanese movements was interviewed by LBC TV to talk about his new treaty. His thesis is that there are two types of people in Lebanon (I think he meant youth): the Generation of Peace (*jeel al salam*) and the Generation of Martyrdom (*jeel al shahada*) which is of course a euphemism for the Generation of War. He did not expand much, but this is clearly a repackaging of the March 8th and March 14th division. However, this appellation is much more malicious as it carries intrinsically a value judgment, something the calendar identification does not. It also falsifies the images of these two political factions, by making one of them superior to the other in terms of moral and ethical values.

The 'peaceniks' of Lebanon are calling for a peace that is imposed by the US and Israeli war machine, which we have seen at work in the past month. It is a peace born from the oppression and the massacre of millions. Many among these peaceniks are led by two of the most ruthless warmongers in the world: Samir Geagea and Walid Jumblat both responsible for some of the worst massacres the country has known. When a peace call sounds like falling bombs, and it is brought about by the indiscriminate massacre of women and children and the destruction of a country's infrastructure, then this is not a peace call. This is at best a cry of fear.

As to the Martyrdom Generation, this is a clear reference to the Shi`a and I wish the author had had enough courage to call things by their names. The Lebanese Orientalists are of the worst kind as they have earned their degrees at the Hollywood academy of political sciences and they get their references from Fox. To them, all the Shi`a want is to die as martyrs. It does not occur to them to ask why? It does not occur to them that there are people who are willing to die for dignity, for the right to *live in peace*. The 'peaceniks' religiously celebrate the Lebanese martyr's day every year to remember those who were killed by the Turks before Lebanon was even a country. Some of them celebrate Easter. But do they celebrate the martyrs who fought the French occupation forces in the South in 1920? They don't even know they exist!

The division peace/war is of course loaded with anti Shi`a discrimination and racism: Peace is a sign of 'civilization' while War is a sign of 'primitiveness'. That does not need to be demonstrated or further expanded. In this division of war and peace, the Shi`a are savages (that's common thinking among Lebanese), and the others are enlightened. Others used to mean 'the Christians', but recently the Sunnis and Druzes have been co-opted as honorary civilized people.

The reason I'm addressing this is that this thinking provides a picture of things to expect in post war Lebanon. Hizbullah will continue to grow and its ranks to swell with young Shi'a who were impressed with its military prowess. The other side will hide behind empty and decontextualized concepts such as 'Peace', as if peace was possible with an enemy as brutal, callous, and merciless as Israel on our borders or in our region. I also want to offer Mr. Lawyer another analogy.

For the self appointed white masters of the world, all Arabs and other colored peoples (and that includes the Lebanese), are animals living on a big farm called Earth. Some parts of this farm are reclaimed and cultivated and the resources are well tapped. Other parts are left in a semi-wild state, for the cost of reclamation may be too high or the time has not yet come for full exploitation. On this farm, there are many animals. Some are fully domesticated and live in pens. Others are wild but live in hiding most of the time. They are part of the farm's biodiversity. They are called "Animals."

The behavior of animals fascinates the viewers of *National Geographic* and similar channels. Some may cause no harm but are not cute. These are usually squashed under the shoe. Some might grow to become a nuisance. They are called vermin and are usually exterminated without guilt. Sometimes some of the farm animals escape to one of the wild sides of the farm, where no one has the time to hunt them. They become feral. They increase in number until they are perceived as a threat to the comfort of the masters or to the performance of other animals. A campaign is then started and they are exterminated. On the farm, some might oppose these massacres but they remain a marginalized minority fighting for animal rights.

Individual animals can be nice and make great pets, especially if they are subservient and house-trained (in human terms this means wearing jeans and eating with fork and knife and generally losing one's culture.) They join the 'just like us' category.

And as with all animals, their babies are so cute. Except baby vermin. Ever heard anyone ever call a baby cockroach cute?

In Lebanon today, there are pets that are treated with care and appreciation and are fed some of the best animal food there is. They are sometimes given full citizenship by the masters. They do the master's work, like the dogs that protect the flock against the wolves. There are lots of domesticated animals (say sheep) waiting in their pens to be milked or slaughtered and who look up admiringly at the masters when they deign to address them. These are the Peace Generation. True, they are given peace in their enclosures, and allowed to establish power relations inside the flock, as it keeps them quiet. This goes on until one of them becomes too aggressive, then this animal is culled and replaced with another. There may be a period of unpleasant void until a new more ruthless leader emerges. This is called politics and can sometimes slip into civil war. There can be innocent victims, but they're just animals.

What the masters want most in their pens is Peace. If food distribution (which the animals produce, but they are only given the waste to eat) is late, there is chaos, and the sheep go Baaaaah Baaaaaaah very loud but all of this disappears when the feed trays are filled. Have I told you that many farmers shag their sheep?

Then there are the wild and the feral ones. These can be a problem. Most of the time they live in bands and keep to themselves. They can trespass on some of the cultivated fields and cause damages which are usually insignificant. There is a commonly held wisdom that the population of these animals should not be allowed to grow as they quickly start to act as if they have rights: the right not to be exploited like the other beasts, the right to freely roam the wild parts of the farm, the right to select their leaders and their power relations, to split into smaller groups, to form viable families, to copulate when and how it suits them with whoever suits them.

So from time to time, especially when the masters get very drunk or very sad or very worried about paying their taxes, they go hunting. They organize themselves into posses and mobs and brag about their weapons and ensure superior fire power and bring their pets with them to help sniff out the vermin and they massacre as many of them as they can. They kill everything and bring back some of the carcasses, but leave most to rot in place. Sometimes they use fire, sometimes explosives; all methods are valid and acceptable. The hiding holes are gassed and whole populations annihilated. This is called War on Terror. At home some of the kids protest the killing: it gives them existential anxiety. So the hunters now and then bring back an orphaned baby to give to the kids who turn it into a pet or who play with it a little bit and then get bored with it and it's a real pity how ugly they become when they grow up.

The white masters have eradicated most of the wild and feral species. But from time to time a more organized pack emerges, no doubt as an evolutionary response to so many exterminations. They fight back and bite and hide their families deeper and further. They attack the hunters to divert them from the rest of the pack so as to preserve the species. Many of them die but eventually the pack survives. This is called the Martyr Generation.

August 15, 2006

The war seems to have ended just as it started, totally unexpectedly. Yesterday morning as I was having coffee around 6:00 AM, the MK drones took a few dives over my house, and threw some of their propaganda leaflets. It was pretty scary because it is accompanied by scores of explosions to detonate the leaflets containers at the right altitude. I then went for my usual run and witnessed from the Corniche the air raid on the Manar TV antenna in Keyfoun, the hill overlooking the airport. There was a huge number of people parked by Rawsheh. They were from Dahieh and had chosen to spend their last war night there instead of waiting for the farewell raids by the Israelis. Families with women, children, scores of young men, all getting ready to move back once the clock shows eight, the time when the ceasefire will start.

And it did. Not a single shot fired. As if someone had suddenly switched the war off. By 8:15 there was a traffic jam on the way to the South and in Beirut there was not one taxi left to take people back to Dahieh. I was riding my bike and a family stopped me near my house and asked me jokingly to take them to Chiyah. Throughout the day, people took the road back to their houses. By 10 AM, the first returnees had reached the front lines, some within a hundred meters from the Israelis, who were leaving their positions in scores. Dahieh was still smoldering and volutes of smokes still coming out of the destroyed buildings and people were returning, some to live there and some to check on their houses and on their neighbors. There were huge traffic jams on the South road, and people were literally driving in the wake of the mechanical shovels moving the debris from the road. Thousands of people were also trying to pass the Lebanese Syrian border causing similar congestion. Everybody was cheering for victory and waving Hassan Nasrallah's pictures and Lebanese and Hizbullah flags.

The destruction in Dahieh is beyond description. It looks like pictures of Dresden after the Allied bombing in WWII.

Later I was discussing the situation with R. of Healthy Basket. I think she hates Hizbullah and its consorts. I was saying that the Aounis (Free Patriotic Movement) were holding a very conciliatory discourse and that they had been very helpful to the displaced during the war. She told me that they had lost a very significant part of their support in the Christian areas and that: "The Christians are spitting on General Aoun for his pro-Resistance stance." Now let's make something clear: the FPM of Aoun was not fighting alongside the Resistance. Its position was that the country is under attack by the Israelis and that we ought to support the people who are suffering and the people who are fighting against those who are destroying our country. By 'support' they mean of course moral support. But even this is unacceptable to a large section of the Lebanese society that was—not very secretly—hoping for a decisive Israeli victory to finish with the Shi`a once and for all and send them back to the holes they crawled out of.

Can someone please explain to me how a country is going to be built when half of it supports Israel and the other is ready to die fighting it? I never thought the Christians in Lebanon will drop Aoun just because he did not condemn Hizbullah and side with the U.S. and Israel, or appear to be unconcerned while (like them) sneering under his breath. This is much worse than I thought.

Later last night, Nasrallah came on TV again. Apparently, the cabinet meeting had to be ended as two March 14th ministers (I am told Fatfat and Moawad) were peddling the notion that Hizbullah had been defeated by the Israelis and that they were expecting weapons to be given to the government immediately and Hizbullah disbanded. These guys are such U.S. parrots that they have stopped being able to see what is happening around them. They also made thinly veiled threats that the Government will not provide aid to the victims and to the displaced until Hizbullah disarms. Nasrallah said three important things.

First, he promised all those who have lost their houses to start as of tomorrow on their reconstruction at Hizbullah's expenses. The Resistance will also give the equivalent of one year's rent to all those people whose house was totally destroyed. He also called for people, engineers and others, to volunteer their time and for traders of construction materials not to hoard materials.

The second thing he said in a very serious tone: It was shameful for people to start talking about laying down the arms when Israel still occupies our lands, and that there were people who were trying to give Israel more than she had asked for.

He finally added that we have first to build the nation in which we all feel secure, and then ask for the weapons and not the other way around. These were clearly the words of a man who feels the world is his and that he does not need a government that has nothing to offer and has never offered anything.

I have decided to stop the Fruits and Vegetable Initiative as there are no refugees left. They have all returned to Dahieh or to the South. Instead, I am going to participate in the reconstruction efforts. People's livelihoods have been destroyed, and I will organize a mobile clinic that will go around villages to help people rebuild their livelihoods. I still have some money from the FVI, but I will raise some more. I will call this project 'Land and People.'

Glossary

Aoun, Michel: A veteran Lebanese politician, a Maronite, and head of the Free Patriotic Movement (see below)

'Aounis: Followers of Michel Aoun

Bekaa: The broad, fertile valley that makes up most of eastern Lebanon

Broummana: A mountain resort town not far from Beirut

chador: A simple, all-enveloping garment, covering the hair and the whole body, that is worn by some very observant Muslim women

Dahieh: A group of suburbs on Beirut's southern fringe that are home to many supporters of Hizbullah

Druze: Adherents of a small, secretive offshoot of Islam, many of whom live in the mountains just south-east of Beirut

Fatah: A large and historically influential Palestinian movement that by 2006 had tied its fortunes to the success of U.S. diplomacy

Free Patriotic Movement (FPM): A Christian party in Lebanon that advocates reforms and has often acted in alliance with Hizbullah. In the 2005 election the FPM won 21 seats.

Hariri: Generally here this is a reference to Saad al-Hariri, son of the veteran Lebanese politician Rafic Hariri who was assassinated in February 2005

hijab: Headscarf worn by observant Muslim women that hides all the wearer's hair

Hizbullah: An organization that was born in reaction to the military occupation that Israel maintained in South Lebanon, 1982-2000. Hizbullah has had a sizeable bloc in Lebanon's elected parliament since 1992, while it has maintained a military capability designed to counter the military threats that Israel continues to pose to Lebanon.

Jabal 'Amel: Mountainous area in south Lebanon that hosted one of Lebanon's two traditional areas of Shi`a population, dating back to the tenth century C.E.

mana'ish: Delicacy usually eaten for breakfast that is a round of Arabic bread smeared with a mix of olive oil, thyme, and other herbs before it is baked, often in a public oven

Manar TV: Hizbullah's television station

March 8 movement: Alliance of Hizbullah, the FPM, and some smaller parties; named after the date in 2005 of a large demonstration they held in Beirut

March 14 movement: Alliance including Saad al-Hariri, Druze leader Walid Jumblatt, and others; named after the date in 2005 of a large demonstration they held in Beirut

Nasrallah, Hassan: Leader of Hizbullah since 1991

LBC TV: Lebanese Broadcasting Corporation, a private company close to the March 14 movement

Maronite church: The largest of several indigenous Christian churches in Lebanon. The Maronites have dominated the Lebanese government since the era of the post–World War I French mandate over Lebanon but in recent decades they have come under increasing pressure from other sects.

Resolution 1559: Resolution adopted by the UN Security Council in September 2004 at the urging of France and the United States; it called on Syria to withdraw its troops from Lebanon and on Hizbullah to disarm

Shi'a: Adherents of one of the two main streams in Islam. In Lebanon there are ancient Shi'a communities in the Bekaa and in the Jebel 'Amel area of South Lebanon, but since the 1950s many have moved to Beirut.

Souk: A market

UNICEF: The UN Children's Fund

UNSC Resolution 1701: Resolution adopted by the UN Security Council on August 11, 2006 that called for a ceasefire between Israel and Hizbullah, for a complete Israeli withdrawal from Lebanon, and the disarmament of Hizbullah

About
Just World Books
"Timely Books for Changing Times"

This title is being published simultaneously as an e-book and a paperback.

Just World Books produces excellent books on key international issues—and does so in a very timely fashion. Because of the agility of our process, we cannot give detailed advance notice of fixed, seasonal "lists". To learn about our existing and future titles, to download author podcasts and videos, and to buy our books, visit our website: www.justworldbooks.com and check our updates on Facebook and Twitter.

Our first title was published in October 2010. By September 2011 we had published six titles, in addition to this one:

America's Misadventures in the Middle East, by Chas W. Freeman, Jr., with a Foreword by William B. Quandt (October 2010)

Afghanistan Journal: Selections from Registan.net, by Joshua Foust, with a Foreword by Steve LeVine (November 2010)

Gaza Mom: Palestine, Politics, Parenting, and Everything In Between, by Laila El-Haddad, with a Foreword by miriam cooke (November 2010)

A Responsible End? The United States and the Iraqi Transition, 2005–2010, by Reidar Visser (December 2010)

Food, Farming, and Freedom: Sowing the Arab Spring, by Rami Zurayk, with a Foreword by Rashid Khalidi (May 2011)

Where the Wild Frontiers Are: Pakistan and the American Imagination, by Manan Ahmed, with a Foreword by Amitava Kumar (June 2011)

Upcoming plans include a book on China by Chas W. Freeman, Jr.; an atlas of the Palestine Question, published in coordination with the Applied Research Institute, Jerusalem (ARIJ); and a book on relations among Turkey, Israel, and the United States, to be edited by William B. Quandt.

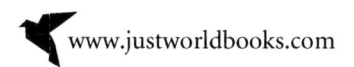

www.justworldbooks.com